T0002266

BEACH COMBING

Cultivate Mindful Moments by the Shore

By Sadie Small

Cover Art by Laura Page
Interior Illustrations by Liana Jegers

BEACH
COMBING

CHRONICLE BOOKS
SAN FRANCISCO

POCKET NATURE SERIES

Text copyright © 2023 by **SADIE SMALL**.

Library of Congress Cataloging-in-Publication Data available.

ISBN 978-1-7972-1792-5

Manufactured in China.

MIX
Paper | Supporting
responsible forestry
FSC™ C136333

Series concept and editing by **CLAIRE GILHULY**.
Series design by **LIZZIE VAUGHAN**.
Cover art by **LAURA PAGE**.
Interior illustrations by **LIANA JEGERS**.

Typeset in Albra, Benton Sans, Caslon.

10 9 8 7 6 5 4 3 2 1

Chronicle books and gifts are available at special quantity discounts to corporations, professional associations, literacy programs, and other organizations. For details and discount information, please contact our premiums department at corporatesales@chroniclebooks.com or at 1-800-759-0190.

Chronicle Books LLC
680 Second Street
San Francisco, California 94107
www.chroniclebooks.com

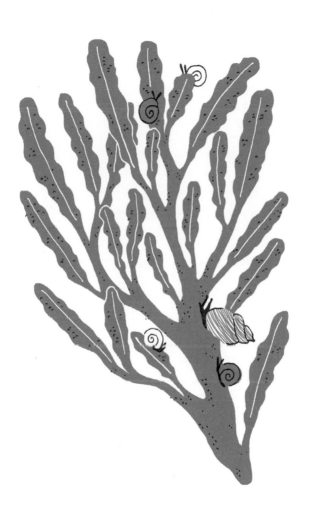

CONTENTS

INTRODUCTION 9

I.
How to Beachcomb 19

II.
Beach Finds 25

III.
What We Can Learn
from the Beach 117

RESOURCES 126

The VOICE OF THE SEA is seductive; never ceasing, WHISPERING, clamoring, murmuring, inviting the soul to wander for a spell in ABYSSES OF SOLITUDE; to lose itself in mazes of INWARD CONTEMPLATION.

—Kate Chopin, from *The Awakening*

INTRODUCTION

I f you're like me, you love the ocean and its inhabitants. You know that a walk on the beach can reveal myriad treasures. What you might not know is what those treasures are called and how they fit into the larger puzzle of the natural world—and that's okay. This book will show you where to begin and how to find joy in all the beach has to offer simply by taking a closer look and by listening to your senses.

The act of beachcombing is as it sounds: "combing"—or exploring, searching—the beach for unique and interesting finds. Sometimes you might add your shoreline treasures to a collection at home, other times, the discoveries you come across are better left in their environment.

Instead of thinking of beachcombing as a way to bolster a prized collection—though it can be that—think of it instead as an opportunity to get outside, listen to the crashing waves, feel the sea breeze on your skin, and observe all the marvelous creatures that reside in our wide world.

No matter what beach you live near, the coast is teeming with life. It might not be obvious at first glance, but look a little closer, peer into the tidepools, watch the waves retreat into the sea, and you'll see it. Tiny little beings going about their business; stunning remnants of life, like castaway shells and egg casings; and remarkable inanimate discoveries, such as sea glass, can be found on the shore. These things exist all around us—we just have to pause long enough to notice them.

Another magical thing about the beach is that it's always changing. In a few hours, the tide will rise or fall, the wind will shift, and the temperature will change. In the coming days, weeks, and months, storms will come and go, and the seasons will pass. Each time you visit the beach, whether it's three hours or three months in between, it will look completely different. Every trip can offer you something new to learn, a chance to add to your understanding of the world around you. There will be novel things to discover, and it's okay if you don't know what all of them are. The important thing is to slow down and admire the wild and ever-changing environment of the beach and the life that survives there beneath the tide, the waves, the wind, and the sun.

Growing up in the Southern California desert, I didn't become intimately acquainted with the sea until I went to college to study ecology at the University of California, San Diego. Sure, I'd taken the occasional trip to the beach with friends, but I didn't fall in love with the coastal ocean until I could see a sliver of it from my dorm room window. On a whim, I took a class in phycology, the study of algae, and wound up studying as an undergraduate in a kelp forest ecology laboratory at Scripps Institution of Oceanography. I was so enamored with the form and function of seaweeds that I continued to study invasive seaweed and get a master's degree in marine ecology at San Diego State University. I've gone on to make restoring natural ocean habitats my life's work—such is the allure of the ocean.

Likewise, you don't have to start young to become a natural historian, an ocean enthusiast, or a beachcomber. The most important characteristics of a beachcomber are simply curiosity and respect. There's a lot to see if you look closely enough, and the tableau changes minute by minute. *Curiosity* can propel you to feel the sand beneath your toes, breathe in the salt-laden air, and bend down to pick up that small, iridescent novelty you've spotted in the surf. It further drives you to inspect your newfound shell and perhaps even to keep it as a new addition to your collection of ocean treasures. *Respect* for the natural world and its inhabitants will keep you safe as you traverse the sea-land boundary of the beach. Keep an eye on the waves and a healthy distance from any birds or mammals you see, and you will preserve both the well-being of coastal habitats and your own safety.

This book doesn't expect you to be or become an expert in everything on the sandy shoreline. Instead, it will show you how to beachcomb and teach you a little bit about what you might find. It will describe different sorts of gastropods (snails and allies), bivalves (oysters and clams), echinoderms (sea stars and urchins), arthropods (crustaceans and allies), cnidarians (jellyfish and the like), and a handful of other interesting finds. It will also give you opportunities to cultivate mindful moments on the coast by tapping into your senses. Most important, this book will instill curiosity and respect for the beach and remind us how privileged we are to walk upon it.

THE SOUNDS
OF THE BEACH

Focusing your attention on the sounds around
you is a powerful way to tap into mindfulness.
By turning off your other senses as best you
can and really *listening*, you can slow your
thoughts, eventually tune them out altogether,
and ground yourself in the here and now.

    The next time you're at the beach, find a
comfortable seat and close your eyes. Settle
into your body. Begin to focus on the sounds
around you. Notice the repetitive crash of
the waves on the shore, the muted roar of
the ocean meeting the earth. How much
time passes between each wave? Consider
how different an incoming, crashing wave
sounds when compared to a retreating one.
How would you describe the sounds of
each? Roaring, smashing, gurgling, swishing,

fizzling? Perhaps you can breathe in sync with the surf. Inhale, crash. Exhale, retreat. Clear your mind and allow the sound of the waves to wash over you.

What else do you hear? Maybe there is an audible sea breeze, or if the weather is turning, maybe it's a whistling wind. Listen for the cries of gulls and other seabirds. Allow their calls to come and go. If there are people nearby, let their words or noises pass by you. When thoughts enter your mind, observe them and let them go, as fleeting as the calls of the birds.

When you feel deeply calm and centered, open your eyes slowly, letting in light. Take a deep breath in through your nose and out through your mouth, reawaken your other senses, and marvel in the beauty of the beach.

When anxious, uneasy,
and bad thoughts come,
I GO TO THE SEA, and the sea
drowns them out
with its GREAT WIDE SOUNDS,
cleanses me with its noise,
and imposes A RHYTHM
upon everything in me
that is bewildered
and confused.

—**Rainer Maria Rilke,** from *Letters of Rainer Maria Rilke, 1892–1910*

I.

HOW TO BEACHCOMB

Anyone can beachcomb, whether you're visiting a favorite seashore or seeing the ocean for the first time. While beachcombing, be mindful of your surroundings and try to notice the everyday details, like the rocks along the water's edge and the birds overhead. By paying close attention to your senses and the world around you, you can begin to enjoy what the beach has to offer to a keen observer. Here are several ways to enhance your beachcombing experience.

▶ **CONSULT A TIDE CHART**

It's often best to visit the beach within two hours of low tide, either before or after, so that more of the beach is exposed for you to explore. For optimal beachcombing, you'll want to visit the intertidal zone, the part of the beach that is exposed by outgoing tides and inundated by incoming tides. At low tide, with the intertidal area revealed and dry, you'll find various marvels you wouldn't otherwise see.

▶ **KNOW YOUR REGULATIONS**
Are you in a Marine Protected Area? If so, check to see if taking shells home is allowed. Some areas are open to visitors but closed to collecting.

▶ **WEAR LAYERS AND SUN PROTECTION**
Layers will keep you comfortable in case the weather changes. Sun protection is essential to shield yourself from the extra solar radiation reflected by the water.

▶ **WALK SLOWLY ALONG THE WATERLINE**
Keep your eyes peeled for interesting finds.

► **BRING A FRIEND**

Especially if the beach is deserted. Two pairs of eyes will be better than one, and a companion means you're safer in case of emergency.

► **PICK UP TRASH AS YOU GO**

Removing plastic and other litter from the beach is the sign of a true beachcomber.

► **DON'T RUSH**

Take your time and use all your senses. Remember, beachcombing isn't just about finding material objects.

► **BRING A CAMERA**

Or use a cellphone to take photos of the items you can't take home from the beach. This can help you identify them later.

► **STAY CURIOUS!**

THE SMELLS
OF THE BEACH

Of the five senses, our olfactory sense may seem to be the least dominant. But smells are important signifiers in our daily lives. Their impact is such that with a single whiff we can instantly be transported to a very specific place or a time long ago. What exactly a smell conjures is unique to each person. Consider what scents are evocative for you—a home-baked apple pie, the jasmine in your parents' garden, the smell of hay in a barn.

Next time you go to the beach, focus on what scents you find there. As you walk along the sand, breathe deeply and appreciate the salty overtones of the ocean air. Chances are you can find other notes in the perfume of the sea, too—the seaweed washed ashore, the

potent scent of marine life, the sweet fra-
grance of sunscreen.

Do any of these seaside smells evoke
something for you? Perhaps a memory—a
certain coastal destination or a beach day from
your childhood. Or maybe it's more ineffable
than that, a feeling of nostalgia, wistfulness,
connectedness, or peace. If it's a happy memory or a positive emotion, hold it in your mind.

As you inhale, take in all the smells of the
beach. Try not to label them as good or bad.
Simply sniff the air and embrace whatever it
is that comes to mind. Then exhale to let it all
wash away.

There for some time
he enjoyed the
<u>FRESH BREEZE</u> which
played on his brow,
and listened to the
dash of the waves
on the beach, that
left against the rocks
a <u>LACE OF FOAM</u> as white
as silver.

—**Alexandre Dumas,** from *The Count of Monte Cristo*

II.

BEACH FINDS

The shoreline is a trove of treasures, from moon snails to sea urchins to hydrozoans. This chapter describes more than twenty common beach finds to help you identify new discoveries on your next adventure. On the next page you'll find an at-a-glance list of all the marvels that appear in these pages—use this to quickly find what you're after.

29
Gastropods

ABALONE 31

SLIPPER SNAILS 35

MOON SNAILS.. 37

OTHER SNAILS.. 41

43
Bivalves

MUSSEL SHELLS 45

OYSTERS... 47

SCALLOPS... 51

CLAMS... 55

59
Echinoderms

SAND DOLLARS....................................... 61

SEA URCHINS.. 65

SEA STARS... 69

73
Arthropods

HORSESHOE CRABS 75

MOLE CRABS 79

TRUE CRABS 83

87
Cnidarians

HYDROZOANS 89

GORGONIANS 93

JELLIES 97

101
Other Interesting Finds

SEAWEED & WRACK 103

CHITON SHELL PLATES 107

SHARK & SKATE EGG CASES 111

SEA GLASS 113

GASTROPODS

Molluscs are any of a large group of invertebrate animals that include snails, slugs, octopuses, squid, clams, and mussels. The most diverse group of molluscs are the gastropods, or snails and slugs. Common characteristics of marine gastropods include a soft, un-segmented body that is usually protected by a coiled shell; and specialized, metallic teeth called radulae. They also have a muscular foot that allows them to move around or anchor in one place. Many of the shells you find while beachcombing will be snail shells, and therefore gastropods.

ABALONE

ABALONE

A balone are marine snails, and their shells are some of the most beautiful items you can find on the beach. The mother-of-pearl lining on the inside of their shells, also known as the nacre, is used in jewelry around the world.

In North America, these large sea snails are limited to the West Coast, where you can find up to seven species. Each species has a unique shell color and shape that tells you something about where that animal lives and what it eats. For example, white abalone live in deep, relatively calm water, so their shells are thin and delicate. Meanwhile, red abalone live in shallow, rough water like tidepools, and have very thick, robust shells. Over time, as abalone get bigger, they grow new shell.

While alive, abalone use their large, muscular foot to cling onto rocks and move around slowly, munching on seaweed. All abalone eat seaweed, and it often shows on their shell—for example, red stripes or tints on the outside of the shell mean that the abalone eats red seaweed. Abalone are cryptic, meaning they are especially good at hiding— in fact, they often look like just another rock. Their strong foot and clever disguise help protect them from predators like octopuses.

In addition to their beautiful shells, abalone are also a culinary delicacy. Native tribes have sustainably harvested abalone for thousands of years. In the mid to late 1900s, recreational and commercial abalone fisheries boomed in California. Fishing was so prolific that we drove many species of this snail to the brink of extinction. Today, only a handful of farms produce abalone for sale as food, and wild harvest is prohibited.

Efforts are underway to use aquaculture (the cultivation of aquatic animals and plants) to breed abalone in captivity and release them back into their natural habitats. Currently, there are more endangered white abalone living in captivity than in the wild! A group of researchers, farmers, aquariums, and regulatory agencies are working together to save this species and restore its wild populations.

The rarity of wild abalone makes finding their shells even more thrilling. When you do find them, they're often broken up into pieces from tumbling around among the rocks, sand, and surf. Because the snail is no longer living in the shell, it's okay to take an abalone shell home and add it to your collection. Be mindful, however, that you are not in a protected area—some beaches do not allow collection of abalone shells. Whether you find a whole shell or just a small part, an iridescent abalone shell is sure to delight.

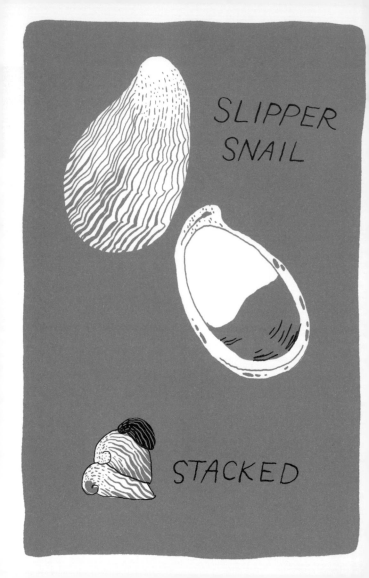

SLIPPER
SNAIL

STACKED

SLIPPER SNAILS

S lipper snail shells are a common
beachcombing find along the Atlantic
and Gulf coasts, where they are a
native species (though you can sometimes
find them on the Pacific coast too, since
they were accidentally brought over with
shipments of oysters in the 1800s).

Slipper snails have a single, oval-shaped
shell with a ledge on the underside that
holds their internal organs and a muscular
foot, which helps them attach to hard objects.
Turned upside-down, you can see that these
shells are aptly named—they look just like a
little slipper. While alive, these snails attach to
rocks or other slipper snails. In fact, they tend
to form long, curving stacks of snails. They live
together this way as adults for a very specific
reason—but let's start at the beginning.

Imagine you're a baby slipper snail. You start your life as a free-swimming pelagic larva—a microscopic baby that swims in the currents of the open ocean. When it comes time to metamorphose, or transform into an adult, you find a nice rock to call home. You settle onto the rock and develop your hard shell and reproductive organs. Surprise, you're male! (Fun fact: All slipper snails are protandrous, meaning that they start off their lives as males and become female later in life.) Over time, you grow larger, and another young snail settles on your shell. That new snail becomes a male as it develops, and you transform into a female. Suddenly, you have found a mate. This process repeats itself until a large stack of snails forms. All of the largest snails on the bottom of the stack are female, the smallest snails on the top of the stack are male, and the middle of the stack are in the process of changing.

If you find a single slipper snail shell, it is most likely empty and would make a great souvenir! If you see a stack of snails, however, they're still alive and you should leave them be.

MOON SNAILS

Moon snails are conspicuous inhabitants of sandy shores. Their shells are rounded, spiraling, tan-colored, and up to 5.5 inches [14 cm] long. When the snail's large foot (the slimy base) is extended, it can fill with water and almost envelop the whole shell, stretching to 12 inches [30 cm] long! This makes them one of the largest snails on Earth, after some species of abalone.

Moon snails are voracious predators, feeding mostly on bivalves and other molluscs Instead of using their toothy radulae (which is like a rough tongue with tiny teeth) to scrape algae, like abalone and slipper snails do, moon snails use their radulae to drill into the shells of their prey and slurp out the soft contents.

The moon snail's shell isn't the only interesting beachcombing find they provide. In

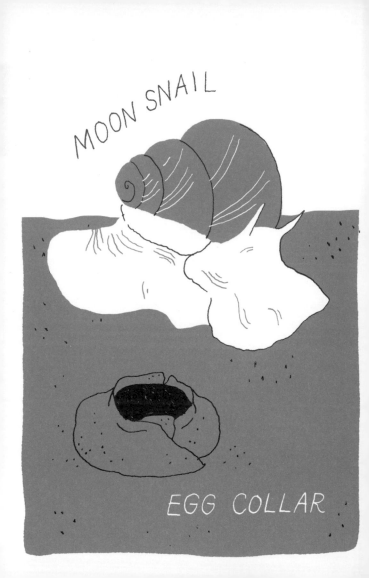

MOON SNAIL

EGG COLLAR

spring and summer, you may find moon snail
eggs, which are encased in a collar-shaped
structure made of sand and mucus. This is
because the female moon snail covers her foot
in mucus and a layer of sand, then lays her
eggs, which she covers in another layer of sand.
When she moves, the unique collar shape
is left behind. Seeing one on the beach, you
might think it's trash, but don't disturb it—
thousands of tiny moon snail babies are inside!

Like most snails, moon snails grow in a
spiral around a central axis, called the colu-
mella. This results in a gap in the shell right
in the middle of the spiral called an umbilicus,
or belly button. This belly button is so distinct
that it can help tell different species apart.
Next time you pick up a moon snail shell, turn
it so the large opening, where its foot should
be, faces you and the smallest part of the
spiral points up. Look to the left of the large
opening and you will see the indentation of
the umbilicus.

PERIWINKLE

COWRIE

CONCH

OLIVE

TURBAN

OTHER SNAILS

There are myriad other little snail shells you will find on the beach. From conical periwinkles and turban snails to cylindrical olives and cowries to ornamental conchs, there's a magnificent diversity of snails. Many of the shells you will find on the beach come from elsewhere, usually from nearby rocky intertidal and sub-tidal areas where the snails lived while alive. Once the snails leave their shells, these little treasures wash up along the beach with the push of the waves.

These shells are often empty and can make excellent souvenirs, but as always, don't take home any shells that still have inhabitants!

BIVALVES

The bivalves are a group of molluscs that include mussels, clams, oysters, and scallops. They have two shells, connected by a hinge, that enclose their bodies. Bivalves are filter feeders, meaning that to eat, they pull water through their bodies, filtering out food and other particles with their gills. Bivalves are probably the second most common types of shells you will find on the beach, after snail shells.

MUSSEL

MUSSEL SHELLS

Many of us are familiar with mussels as seaside cuisine. It's also common to find the shells of these bivalve molluscs on the beach, deeply blue or black and white on the outside with a thin layer of mother of pearl on the inside.

Before we see them on our plates or on the sand, mussels attach to wave-exposed rocks in the intertidal zone, clinging to rocks with tough fibers called byssal threads. Byssal threads, which we commonly call beards and remove before eating, are simultaneously stretchy and strong, like a tendon sheathed in iron-like fibers.

Mussels make tasty snacks for predators like gulls, sea stars, and even snails called whelks. While gulls and sea stars remove mussels partially or wholly from the rocks, whelks have their meal without dealing with pesky byssal threads. They use a specialized drill to breach the shell, and then emit an enzyme that dissolves the mussel's body into liquid that they subsequently slurp up.

Like many other bivalves, mussels are filter feeders, meaning they find their food by filtering the water flowing past them. When they're submerged at high tide, mussels pass water through their gills, allowing them to breathe. What's interesting, however, is that mussel gills multitask in a way that fish gills cannot. While mussel gills filter oxygen out of the water to breathe, they also catch phytoplankton and other particulates to eat. Those resourceful gills are breathing and eating (or, more accurately, filtering for food) simultaneously! Mussels can even consume harmful bacteria like *E. coli*; a single mussel can clean up to 6 gallons [27 liters] of water per day.

Next time you pick up a beautiful mussel shell, think about the life it lived protecting coastal waters. And check for a small drill hole from a whelk—this could be the perfect way to make your beach find into a pendant!

OYSTERS

Like mussels and scallops, oysters are known best for their culinary uses. In North America, there are two native species—Olympic and Atlantic oysters—and one common species that was introduced from the eastern Pacific Ocean for farming—the Pacific oyster.

Oysters have irregular teardrop–shaped white shells that may show stripes of purple and brown on the outside and a pearlescent lining on the inside. They are filter feeders, like other bivalves, and grow on hard surfaces like rocks, jetties, or other oysters. Atlantic and Pacific oysters are commonly found both farmed and in the wild on their respective coasts, usually in estuaries and bays. On both coasts, Indigenous peoples have been farming and harvesting native oysters for millennia. A

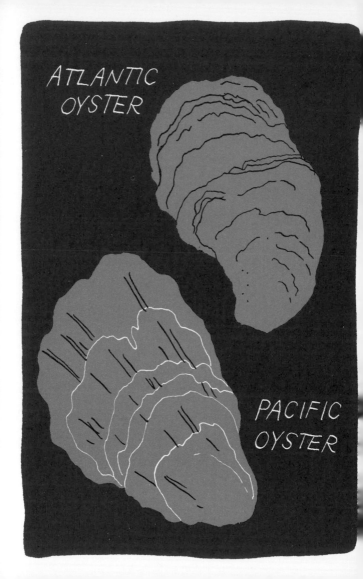

ATLANTIC OYSTER

PACIFIC OYSTER

keen observer can sometimes find collections of discarded shells, called middens, near the beach.

Atlantic oysters, in particular, form ecologically important reefs that provide habitat, food, and shelter for countless other animals, including many species of fish, crustaceans, and molluscs. Oyster reefs are especially critical habitats for juvenile critters because they have lots of nooks and crannies where young animals can take refuge from hungry predators like crabs and adult fish. Oyster reefs have other benefits to natural ecosystems and humans too. Reefs decrease the effects of high waves and storm surge, protecting beaches and coastal communities. Oyster reefs also clean seawater even more effectively than mussels do—one Atlantic oyster can filter up to 50 gallons [227 liters] of water per day! In estuaries like the Chesapeake Bay, oyster removal of phytoplankton, toxins, metals, and sediments from the water also makes it clearer. This allows more light to penetrate to the seafloor and reach important aquatic plants like seagrasses. Because oyster reefs have so many advantages for people and the environment alike, there are efforts on both coasts to restore historical and pre-historical populations of these species.

Consider how remarkable it is that these small, unassuming organisms can have such a huge impact on things much bigger than themselves. We should never underestimate our own capacity or that of other beings!

Although oysters are not the most photogenic of the seashells you'll find on the beach, hopefully knowing some of their natural history gives their oddly shaped shells new shine.

SCALLOPS

If you close your eyes and envision a shell, chances are you think of a scallop. Scallops are bivalve molluscs with two rounded, ridged shells connected by a hinge. Unlike many other bivalves, scallops cannot close their shells completely, so they do not survive for long out of the water. While they may not be as hardy to air exposure as other bivalves, scallops have other interesting adaptations.

What we think of as a scallop in culinary terms is actually just the animal's large, well-developed adductor muscle. This muscle keeps the shells together, and also allows many species of scallop to swim freely. This ability to swim is unique among adult bivalves. To swim, a scallop sucks water into its body cavity and uses the adductor muscle to quickly close

SCALLOP

its shell. This rapid motion of the shell forces water out like a jet, which propels the scallop backward through the water. Most of the time, scallops swim slowly, unless they're threatened by a predator, in which case they can move at the rate of 14 inches [37 cm] per second! Scallops have up to two hundred bright blue eyes lining the open edges of their shells that allow them to sense a predator by detecting light and motion in their environment.

Next time you find a scallop shell, run your fingers along the distinct ridges that radiate from the narrow hinge to the wide lip of the shell. The shell may feel relatively smooth or it may be bumpy. See if you can feel and count the annual growth lines that run parallel to the deeper ridges and grooves; one of these lines equates to one year of life. Some scallops can be up to twenty years old. Can you tell how old yours is?

CLAMS

U nlike many shells you find that are washed ashore from different envi-ronments like rocky reefs, clams live in the soft, sandy beach. Instead of attaching to hard things like oysters and mussels do, or swimming like scallops, clams burrow into sand and mud. They either extend a tube-like structure, or siphon, to the surface of the sand to breathe and filter feed, or they burrow upward to feed on the beach surface. Like many molluscs, clams have large muscular feet, which they use to dig instead of attach to rocks.

One common type of clam is the bean clam or coquina. You may not notice them at first, since they're usually less than 1 inch [2.5 cm] long. Bean clams are shaped like a scalene triangle, where each side is a different length, and their coloring can range from pastel sandy colors to jewel tones. These clams can be found in the swash zone, the area of the beach where the waves wash up and retreat. Usually, many bean clams live close together, so what may look like numerous small disturbances in the flow of an ebbing wave may be an aggregation of hundreds or thousands of them. Once you've found a few, crouch down in the sand and look along the beach, and you'll likely notice numerous others. This abundant resource is important for the beach ecosystem, as bean clams feed predators like seabirds. They are edible by humans too—bring a colander and bucket to sift them from the sand if you want to take a treat home with you. Bonus: Their shells are the perfect size to make into jewelry like earrings.

Another interesting and common type of clam is the razor clam. This group gets its name from the Atlantic species' shape, which looks like an old-fashioned barber's straight razor, though Pacific species are more robustly oval-shaped. Razor clams are typically brown or amber in color and may reach lengths of 12 inches [30 cm]. They are fast burrowers due to their strong muscular foot. Like most bivalves, they are filter feeders, but their siphons are so large that they cannot be retracted into their shells. If you see a vertical spurt of water coming from the damp beach, you have found a razor clam.

Razor clams are known for an unusual body part called a zipper formed by the mantle along the edge of their shells. This zipper helps the clam form new shell as it grows!

Like bean clams, live razor clams can be eaten; in fact, people commonly harvest razor clams in the Pacific Northwest using a shovel or clam gun and bring them home for a delicious feast.

ECHINODERMS

Echinoderms are a group of exclusively ocean-dwelling invertebrates that include sea stars, sea urchins, sand dollars, and sea cucumbers. They are characterized by radial symmetry, or having bodies where one half is the mirror image of the other half. Unlike molluscs, they do not have shells; rather, their skeleton-less bodies are protected by tests (hard shells) and spines, either within their tissues, as in sea stars, or surrounding their bodies, like sea urchins and sand dollars.

ECCENTRIC
SAND DOLLAR

ARISTOTLE'S
LANTERN

SAND DOLLARS

Sand dollars are an iconic beachcombing find. Washed ashore, we usually only see their test, or exoskeleton, which is as white as bone after tumbling in the surf and sand. When alive, however, sand dollars are coated in velvety spines and tube feet that can be violet, purple, blue, or green depending on the species. Sand dollars are a type of flattened sea urchin, so they share many anatomical and life history characteristics, but they feed very differently. Instead of scraping at their food to eat it, sand dollars stand upright on the sandy seafloor and filter feed from the water flowing past. Their tube feet aren't made for walking—rather, their purpose is to catch tiny animals and algae known as plankton and move the prey toward their mouth, which consists of a set of grinding plates known as an Aristotle's lantern. (The fourth-century philosopher Aristotle thought sea urchin jaws looked like lanterns, and we have known them as Aristotle's lanterns ever since.)

But, if it's a windier day and the waves are rough (or maybe there's a hungry sea star or octopus nearby), a sand dollar uses its spines to hunker down. Sand dollars will lie flat and push those spines into the sand below, anchoring into the sea floor. To avoid being washed ashore, they may even use their tube feet to eat sand grains and weigh themselves down. But if this doesn't work, you might come across a live sand dollar up on the beach (you'll know because it won't be white). If that happens, you'll want to return it to the water.

The distinctive five-petaled flower design on sand dollar tests alludes to their evolution—though they may not look similar at first glance, sand dollars are related to sea stars. Both have five-fold radial symmetry, meaning their bodies are arranged around a central axis like pieces of a pie. In sand dollars, the flower design is lined with tiny pores that allow the animal to breathe. Here, their special tube feet serve yet another purpose: They act like our lungs. The tube feet poke through the tiny pores into the seawater to inhale oxygen and exhale carbon dioxide. Think of this next time you find a sand dollar shell on the beach. Feel each tiny groove in the test with your thumb as you trace the design and focus on your own breath. This beautiful shell may have lived up to a decade before reaching your hands.

SEA URCHINS

A sea urchin test is a beautiful, delicate addition to any beachcomber's collection of shells and other ocean trinkets. At first glance, urchins look like pin cushions. Anatomically, they are like spherical sand dollars with pointy spines. They can grow to between 1 and 5 inches [2.5 to 12.5 cm] wide, depending on the species. The largest species of sea urchin is the red urchin, which grows on the Pacific coast. This species can shelter other smaller species, like the purple urchin, from predators using its extra-long spines.

Urchins typically live in rocky areas like tidepools, reefs, and kelp forests, where they eat seaweed and microalgae. Urchins are such voracious eaters that, if there aren't enough predators like lobsters or sea otters, they can decimate kelp forests, transforming a lush ecosystem teeming with life into a rocky, empty urchin barren. Any little bit of food, including microscopic baby kelps, are immediately mowed down, making it difficult for the kelp forest ecosystem to regrow and recover.

Despite their big appetites, sea urchins can live for very long periods of time without eating. When an urchin has plenty of food, it grows roe, or reproductive organs—this is the delicacy we call uni in a sushi restaurant. When the urchin is starving, however, it can reabsorb those nutrients. If you crack open a starving purple urchin, instead of bright orange roe lining the interior grooves of its shell, it will be empty inside.

On the north coast of California, marine heatwaves and urchin grazing have led to the collapse of kelp forest ecosystems, which has also threatened the culturally important red abalone fishery in the area. Former abalone divers are teaming up with scientists to harvest these "zombie" urchins in order to protect the underwater forests. To make this restoration venture more financially attractive, some urchin ranchers are known to fatten up these zombie urchins on land so they can sell the roe to restaurants.

A live sea urchin will still have its spines. Unless you know the species is safe, it's best not to touch an urchin as some species can be venomous. However, an empty urchin test—which you can identify by its lack of spines—is safe to take home. Because of its graceful and elegant structure, you won't often find one completely intact; if you do, it's a real treasure.

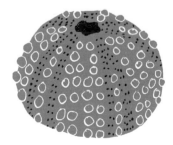

SEA
STARS

SEA STARS

S ea stars are a favorite find for beach-combers of all ages. (Sea stars are often called starfish, but because these critters aren't related to fish, it's more accurate to call them sea stars.) Though they don't have shells you can take home, they're beautiful and enigmatic creatures that come in a variety of shapes, sizes, and colors. The classic sea star we think of has five arms, but some species can have many more, like the nine-armed sea star that can be found on the Atlantic coast of North America. Most species of sea star have the same number of arms throughout their lifespan, but not all. The sunflower sea star, found on the Pacific coast, starts life with five or six arms, and grows more with age—up to twenty-four—with a maximum arm span of over 3 feet [1 meter]! If a sea star loses an arm, it can regenerate, so don't worry if you see a lopsided star. Sea stars are commonly gray, white, orange, or purple, depending on the species.

Up to fifteen thousand tube feet act like tiny suction cups on the underside of each arm of a sea star and allow it to move around rocky reefs or the sandy seafloor. These tube feet can secrete a strong sticky substance to keep the sea star anchored to rocks despite crashing waves. When the sea star wants to move, however, the tube feet release a solvent that allows them to detach from the rock. Though they don't swim, sea stars can use their tube feet to move relatively quickly, with larger stars often moving more quickly than smaller ones. For example, the sunflower sea star can move almost 40 inches [100 cm] per minute.

Sea stars are predatory, meaning they eat other animals. They often eat slower-moving species like sea urchins, or sessile, non-moving species like mussels or corals. They find their food through chemoreception, which is similar to the human sense of smell. Like other echinoderms, sea stars have sharp jaws called an Aristotle's lantern. Unlike other echinoderms, however, they evert their stomachs, or turn them inside out, while eating. This means that the stomach comes out of their mouth and surrounds their prey to digest it rather than bringing the prey into their bodies.

At the very tip of their arms, sea stars have black or red eyespots. Though they can't witness the world the way we do, these eyespots allow them to sense light and dark. This lets them receive important information about their surroundings like the presence of predators or a good dark nook to hide in.

If you see a sea star at the beach or on a rock, resist the urge to pick it up. This is a beach find that isn't made for taking home. Let the sighting of a sea star remind you that beachcombing isn't just about collecting treasures; it's an exercise in mindful observation too.

ARTHROPODS

The arthropods are the most diverse and speciose group of animals on Earth! They range from insects to chelicerates like horseshoe crabs to crustaceans like shrimp, true crabs, and lobsters. Arthropods have external skeletons, or exoskeletons, and segmented bodies where each segment has a pair of appendages. To grow, arthropods must molt, or shed their old exoskeletons for a new, larger exoskeleton to form. What we most often find while beachcombing are these molts—the pieces of the exoskeleton rather than the remains of whole arthropods.

HORSESHOE CRAB

HORSESHOE CRABS

Despite their name, horseshoe crabs aren't true crabs; rather, they are an ancient group more closely related to other arthropods like terrestrial scorpions and spiders than they are to crabs. Horseshoe crabs have existed on the Earth for about 250 million years with minimal evolutionary change, earning them the moniker of living fossils. Their bodies consist of a main body section of exoskeleton, called a carapace, that is beige and hoof-shaped, under which are five pairs of jointed legs, a pair of feeding pincers, and a tail spike. Horseshoe crabs use their tail spike, or telson, like the rudder of a ship to help steer them as they swim, and to help flip them right-side up if they end up on their backs.

Horseshoe crabs have nine eye-like organs, including a pair of compound eyes on their carapace and photosensitive regions on their telsons. (Compound eyes are common among crustaceans and insects; they can see a wider angle but have poorer image quality than human single-aperture eyes.) Different eyes have different functions; for example, only some sense visible light, while others sense ultraviolet light. Horseshoe crabs use their compound eyes to find mates, and the photosensitive array on their telson to tell whether it's night or day.

Though horseshoe crabs live in the deep waters off the Atlantic coast, annual springtime spawning events bring them into the shallows, where we can observe their mating ritual. At high tide in late spring, droves of horseshoe crabs congregate near the shore. Smaller male horseshoe crabs hitch a ride up the beach on larger female crabs, where the female lays up to four thousand tiny green eggs in a nest at a time and the male fertilizes them. (A single female may lay as many as ninety thousand eggs in a day!) The eggs hatch several weeks later. Unlike many marine babies, young horseshoe crabs don't go through many different body forms before maturing; they look much like smaller adults. Young horseshoe crabs are an important food source for seabirds, fish, sea turtles, and other marine invertebrates.

Horseshoe crabs provide an important resource for humans too. We capture horseshoe crabs and use their blood to derive limulus amebocyte lysate (LAL), which helps us test for bacterial contamination in pharmaceuticals. Thanks to these ancient sea creatures, we can ensure our medicine is safe for consumption. Next time you walk along the Atlantic shoreline, keep in mind how the horseshoe crab supports the circle of life, both in the natural ecosystem and in human health.

DEPRESSIONS
IN SWASH ZONE

MOLE CRAB

MOLE CRABS

L ike horseshoe crabs, mole crabs, also called sand crabs or sand fleas, are not true crabs. In fact, a mole crab is more closely related to a lobster than to a true crab. Mole crabs are pale-colored, egg-shaped crabs that may reach up to 1 inch [2.5 cm] long and can camouflage well into their sandy habitat of the swash zone. They have strong telsons, or tails, to dig and to anchor themselves in the sand beneath the waves.

These small crabs cannot bite or pinch you. Unlike many other animals, female mole crabs are larger than males, which comes in handy when it's time to breed. Up to forty thousand bright orange fertilized crab eggs incubate on the underside of the female's body, while her telson folds underneath to protect the precious cargo. After about a month of

incubation, the eggs hatch and release plank-
tonic larvae, meaning that the baby crabs swim
in the ocean for the first part of their lives.

To feed, mole crabs move up and down
the beach with the tide, crouching near the
surface of the sand with their antennae
extended to catch plankton in the surf. Mole
crabs face away from the ocean as they feed,
gathering most of their food as receding waves
wash over them. As you're beachcombing, if
you see small *V*-shaped depressions in the
sand in the swash zone, you may have found
mole crabs! Mole crabs are a favorite treat for
seabirds, fish, and true crabs. Not only are they
an important food source in the sandy beach
ecosystem, but they also make good bait for
fishermen. If you come across these little crabs
during your walk, observe them, but don't pick
them up. Leave them be and simply watch
them feed and burrow as the waves rush back
and forth over the sand.

ATLANTIC
BLUE CRAB

TRUE CRABS

T rue crabs look a lot like their mole crab and lobster cousins, but they have flatter carapaces, or abdomens, and shorter tails. Examples of common true crabs are blue, rock, and Dungeness crabs. Wondering why so many animals are called crab but aren't "true crabs?" It's because of a phenomenon called carcinization, where many crustaceans have evolved over time to have a crab-like body plan, even though they don't all share the same common ancestor. Carcinization is an example of convergent evolution, a process where unrelated organisms independently evolve similar characteristics. Another good example of convergent evolution is the development of wings in both bats and birds—totally unrelated animals that evolved similar structures to meet similar goals.

If you find the body of a crab in the sand, there's a good chance that it's just a molt, or the exoskeleton left behind when a crab grows larger, rather than a dead crab. Young crabs molt multiple times a year while they're growing quickly, and adult crabs molt about once a year. In fact, some crab species, like Dungeness on the West Coast, tend to molt all at once—females in the spring, males in the late summer—so if you see many crab exoskeletons on the beach, don't worry. You're not witnessing a mass mortality event, just the normal passage of time.

One spectacular species of crab is the Atlantic blue crab, an East Coast favorite in North America. These crabs have greenish carapaces (shells) and brilliant blue legs. You can tell males and females apart easily— males are bigger, up to 9 inches [23 cm] in width, and females are a bit smaller with bright red pincers. Most species of crabs are only capable of walking sideways, but the blue crab has something else up its sleeve. The last pair of legs are flattened and paddle-like, allowing them to swim!

On the West Coast, Dungeness crab are a prized species. These crabs have purplish carapaces and orange legs and can grow a bit bigger than blue crabs at about 10 inches [25 cm] across. Both blue and Dungeness crabs mate when the female crabs have just molted and have a soft shell. Female blue crabs mate only once in their lives, while Dungeness live through multiple mating seasons. To protect populations of these important crabs, it is illegal to harvest gravid, or egg-bearing, females.

CNIDARIANS

Mostly marine animals, the cnidarians include corals, hydras, jellies, Portuguese men-of-war, sea anemones, and sea fans. Cnidarians have soft bodies, but may also make hard parts, like corals do. Their unifying characteristic is the cnidocyte, a specialized type of cell that allows them to sting prey or predators.

BLUE BUTTON

HYDROZOANS

H ydrozoans are a class of gelatinous, free-floating cnidarians, including by-the-wind sailors, blue buttons, and Portuguese men-of-war. They are holoplankton, meaning that they spend their entire lives in the open ocean. Though these animals may seem large, they are usually made up of a colony of smaller animals with different specialized tasks that comprise the whole organism. Most hydroids have two life stages—the cylinder-shaped polyp stage, where they usually live colonially; and the reproductive, bell-shaped medusa stage, where they are more often free-floating individuals. Because hydrozoans follow ocean currents, species are often cosmopolitan, meaning that they are distributed throughout the Earth's oceans instead of in a particular spot.

One stunning example is the by-the-wind sailor, or velella, a bright blue hydrozoan with a clear fin-shaped sail that lives on the surface of the ocean and uses the wind to move from place to place. In contrast to many hydrozoans, by-the-wind sailors are not colonial animals—they are one large, specialized polyp instead of many small polyps with different functions. When it's time to reproduce, males and females alike asexually "bud off" or produce tiny medusae, which look like miniature jellies, and then descend around 2,000 to 3,000 feet [600 to 900 m] and release an egg and a sperm each. When an egg and sperm combine, a larva is formed and begins the journey of developing into a polyp in the depths. A few months later, timed with phytoplankton blooms in spring or fall, the new polyps ascend to the surface to feed and start the cycle over again.

While their primary food is plankton, both polyp and medusa forms of the by-the-wind sailor also have zooxanthellae, or phytoplankton that live in their cells and contribute to their nutrition. By-the-wind sailors use tentacles to trap their tiny prey, but these tentacles are not dangerous to humans. Strong winds may lead to mass strandings of these animals, coating beaches in blue creatures whose color fades as they're left out in the sun.

Another vibrant hydrozoan is the blue button, sometimes called the blue button jellyfish, though it's not a jelly at all. Blue buttons have a clear central disc that they use to control their buoyancy with sun-shaped rays of azure, or even yellow or purple, polyps radiating outward. This hydrozoan is colonial, and like most cnidarians, uses stinging cells to catch its food as it floats on the surface of the ocean. Blue buttons may be inadvertently stranded on the beach in the same way as by-the-wind sailors are. If you find one, don't touch it—while the sting is not fatal, it can be irritating to your skin. Instead, take a moment to admire the beautiful coloration of this bottlecap-sized animal.

COMMON SEA FAN

GORGONIANS

G orgonians, also known as soft corals or sea fans, are related to the reef-forming true coral species found in tropical oceans. They are usually brightly colored in hues of purple, pink, orange, red, and yellow. Gorgonians are colonial animals that are upright and flexible, resembling finely branched, flattened shrubs. Their fibrous "skeleton" is made of either gorgonin or calcium carbonate, giving structure to the layer of polyps covering its entire surface. They live attached to hard bottoms, like the "living rock" of a coral reef in shallow seas or a rocky patch of the deep sea, and eventually wash up onto the beach at the end of their lives for us to marvel.

Gorgonians have eight-fold symmetry—each polyp is cylindrical with eight tentacles and an eight-segmented body. The overall effect of these sea fans is intricate and fractal-like, with branches spreading out in a single plane perpendicular to the direction of prevailing water flow. This way, the delicate network of polyps can catch passing plankton. Like their hard coral cousins, gorgonians can create habitat for other species, like brittle stars, sea stars, sponges, and algae. Worldwide, some sea fans even have close relationships with fish, namely pygmy seahorses that mimic the appearance of their gorgonian hosts!

If you find a gorgonian on the beach, there's no need to worry that it will sting you. Since it has come detached from its hard-bottom home, the animal likely is no longer living, and makes a spectacular beach-combing souvenir. As with most finds, they're delicate, so take care. You may want to leave the specimen in a covered area outside for a few weeks as it fully dries out to avoid any lingering smells. Once it's been properly dried, you can keep a sea fan to remind you of the intricate nature of ocean ecosystems.

JELLIES

J ellies, commonly known as jellyfish, are a familiar sight marooned on beaches. In life, they're holoplankton (open ocean–dwelling) with bell-shaped bodies and cascading tentacles. Jellies range widely in size, with bell widths ranging from less than 1 inch [2.5 cm] to 7 feet [2.1 m], and tentacle lengths from minuscule to 120 feet [36.5 m] long. Like hydrozoans, they tend to be cosmopolitan species, moving freely throughout the world's oceans. Unlike the hydrozoans, jellies can actively swim by sucking water into their bodies and contracting a ring of muscles around the bell to expel the water, propelling them forward. Like all cnidarians, they have stinging cells, which can be found on their tentacles.

A common jelly sighted on North American beaches on both coasts is the moon jelly.

This jelly is one of the least likely to cause skin irritation if you come into contact with its short tentacles. Moon jellies are translucent white (though sometimes blue or purple!), with bells 2 to 16 inches [5 to 40.5 cm] wide and a characteristic four-leaf clover shape visible in the middle of their bell. This four-leaf clover holds their gonads, or reproductive structures. Moon jellies tolerate low salinity water well, so they are often found in bays and harbors where freshwater is mixed with seawater, though they are also present in the open ocean. If you see a moon jelly on the beach, it may look like a plastic bag. This resemblance is problematic because moon jellies are an important food source for sea turtles, and turtles sometimes consume plastic bags thinking they are jellies. This is just one reason why it's important to pick up litter while you're beachcombing!

Lion's mane jellies are a truly stunning beachcombing find because they're the largest species of jelly in the world, clocking in at 8 feet [2.5 m] wide and 120 feet [36.5 m] long.

Their bells are tan, purple, or red in color; and they have voluminous, mane-like, reddish tentacles that pack a powerful sting. If you find fragments of tentacles onshore, beware, because they will sting you long after they've detached from the jelly. Lion's mane jellies are bioluminescent, meaning that they can glow in the dark due to the presence of special bacteria in their tissues. This glow attracts prey toward their sticky, stinging tentacles. Lion's mane jellies feed on fish, smaller cnidarians including moon jellies, and zooplankton near the surface of the ocean. Like all jellies, they swallow their prey whole and use enzymes to digest it without chewing. Not all fish are food, however—some fish, like jacks, are unaffected by the stinging tentacles and take refuge from predators near the lion's mane jelly. Despite this creature's enormous size, the lion's mane jelly has a lifespan of only one year.

OTHER INTERESTING FINDS

From plant material to skeletons to inanimate objects like sea glass, this section includes a handful of common beach finds that don't neatly fall into other categories.

RED
COMB
WEED

GIANT KELP

SEAWEED & WRACK

I magine walking through a dense forest with a tall canopy, the shade of the trees only letting through the odd sunbeam. Think of the lush understory of small trees, bushes, and vines, and the leaf litter beneath your feet. Out of the corner of your eye, you see a squirrel flicking its tail; you hear bird-song high above. Rich forests like these don't only exist on the land—they live beneath the waves too. Large, canopy-forming species of golden-brown seaweed called kelps form the basis of this habitat, while the understory is filled in by smaller red and green seaweeds. We call these ecosystems kelp forests, or even kelp cathedrals, and they're home to countless fish and invertebrates.

When alive, seaweeds make their energy from sunlight—i.e., photosynthesize—using every part of their bodies, not just their leaf-like fronds. Some have air bladders that buoy them up toward the bright sunlight at the surface, while others lie on the seafloor and sway back and forth with the waves. Unlike land plants, seaweeds don't have roots—instead, they use specialized structures called hold-fasts to anchor themselves to the seafloor and absorb nutrients. Holdfasts can be shaped like round discs or like fingers, and they cling to rocks instead of digging into the sand. Despite their strength, every holdfast eventually meets its match in the form of stormy seas, dislodges, and washes ashore.

Instead of seeing the magnificent kelp forest on the beach, what we see are small bits of plant-like seaweed and tangled heaps of decomposing brown kelp, which are collectively known as wrack. In many places, beaches are groomed to remove this somewhat unpleasant remnant of the torn-up kelp forest. If you dare to look more closely, however, you can see echoes of what once lived under the waves, be it 90-foot- [27.5-meter-] long strands of giant kelp or delicate, fernlike red seaweeds. While seaweed wrack may not be a treasure you take home from the beach, it's an important part of the ecosystem and should be appreciated just the same. Small crustaceans feed on the wrack, and in turn, seabirds like plovers, terns, and sandpipers feed on the crustaceans. Wrack is also part of the experience of the beach—the telltale salty smell that greets you on the shoreline almost certainly includes the scent of washed-up seaweed.

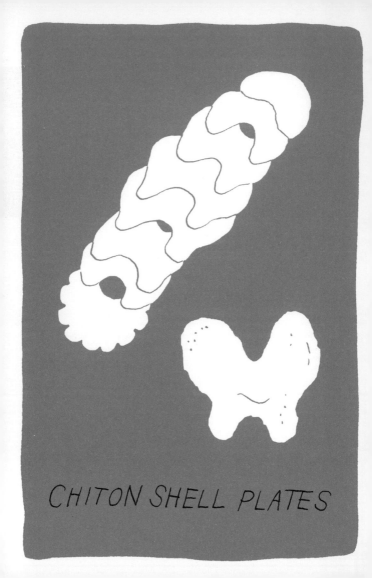

CHITON SHELL PLATES

CHITON SHELL PLATES

Y ou're walking along the beach and you see something triangular and bonelike, so you stoop to pick it up, thinking, *I've found a shark tooth!* Probably not—you've more likely found a shell plate from a chiton, a type of mollusc with eight-segmented shells covering a large muscular foot. Living chitons look very different from the singular, triangular shell plate you find in the sand—they're often clad in pink, orange, and green, and the shell plates may or may not be visible at all.

Before they die and their shell plates wash up on the shore, chitons live on intertidal and subtidal rocky reefs. (Intertidal zones are those that are underwater at high tide but exposed at low tide; subtidal zones are those that always underwater but shallow and close to the shore.) If you see one in a tidepool, you might guess it never moves because it clings so tightly to the rocks. Many smaller species, like the lined chiton, create a "home scar," or a home base, by scraping away layers of rock using their sharp radulae and only leave that haven when they are safe from predation or desiccation (drying out). In the intertidal zone, this means that these chitons only leave their home scar during high tide when they can forage for algae without worrying about losing too much moisture. To eat, they again use their radulae to scour small algae off the rocks. In fact, the chiton radula is one of the hardest and most durable biominerals that we have discovered, containing iron oxides like magnetite to endure relentless grinding against rocks.

One species of chiton stands out from the rest—the gumboot chiton. While most species are visibly armored by their eight shell plates, this species has an orange leathery covering over its shell. At over 1 foot [30 cm] long, it is also about ten times the size of the average chiton species. The size, shape, and color of the gumboot chiton has earned it the nickname *wandering meatloaf*, and it's far less shy than its smaller counterparts. Gumboot chitons are gentle giants, however, and eat the same microalgae as other chiton species.

As with many beach finds, chiton shell plates only tell a fraction of the story that the whole, live animal has to offer. Knowing what the tiny shell plate means, how it fits into the rest of the chiton's armor, and how the chiton fits into the ecosystem can help us better appreciate nature when we visit the beach. Chiton shell plates make excellent mementos of your trip to the coast.

CALIFORNIA
HORN
SHARK
EGG CASE

SKATE
EGG
CASE

SHARK & SKATE
EGG CASES

Often called mermaid's purses, shark and skate egg cases are some of the most bizarre and magical things to find on the beach. They aren't commonly found because most shark species are viviparous, meaning they give birth to live young. Others, like horn sharks, many catsharks, and skates, are oviparous, placing a single egg and its embryo into its own special leathery pouch complete with nourishing yolk. These egg cases are made of collagen, the material that gives structure and elasticity to human joints and skin. After a few weeks, slits open to allow seawater to flow through the egg case, and within a few months (or, for white skates, fifteen months!), the baby shark or skate hatches, and the egg case follows the currents and eventually winds up on the beach for us to see.

Knowing the shark's habitat can tell you a lot about how its egg cases look. Each group of sharks and skate egg cases may be shaped differently. Horn sharks live in rocky reef habitats, and their egg cases are shaped like corkscrews so they can lodge in cracks between rocks. Catsharks also live in rough-bottomed habitats, and their egg cases are rectangular with vine-like tendrils coming off the corners that allow them to tangle up in seaweed. Skates live in sandy habitats, and their rectangular egg cases have long, straight protrusions that anchor the egg cases into soft seafloor.

Chances are, if you're finding a mermaid's purse, the inhabitant is long gone and it's shriveled, brown, and a fraction of its former size. In this case, they make excellent souvenirs! If, however, the egg case is heavy and not broken open, you can pick it up for just a moment and hold it up to the sunlight. If you're very lucky, you may be able to see the heartbeat of an embryo! Then be sure to return it to the ocean as soon as possible. Either way, finding a mermaid's purse is an extra-special experience.

SEA GLASS

Tumbled and smoothed by the relentless sand and surf, sea glass can be a beautiful keepsake from your beachcombing trip. "Genuine" sea glass has a frosted appearance, even though the source glass was clear, because some chemicals present in the original piece have been leached out by seawater. To find sea glass you can take home, you'll want to visit a beach that's more pebbly than sandy, since particle sizes of rocks tend to group together. There's plenty of sea glass on a finer beach, but it's probably only sand-grain-sized!

Sea glass comes from glass discarded by humans, either on purpose or in events like shipwrecks and natural disasters. Places with a high concentration of sea glass usually have a history of waste disposal, like Glass Beach in

GLASS
FISHING FLOAT

Fort Bragg, California. Historically, residents dumped their trash here, which resulted in a high concentration of glass for decades to come. In recent years, glass has become a much less common container type in favor of plastic, so new sea glass isn't created as often. In addition, environmental regulations have reduced the amount of litter on beaches in the United States, so sea glass is a much rarer find today than it was in decades past.

A different item that's even more coveted than sea glass is the glass fishing float. These were first used by Norwegian fishermen in the 1840s, replacing wood or cork floats. Glass floats supported fish nets and lines throughout much of the northern hemisphere, but they are particularly known for their use by Japanese fishermen starting in 1910. These hollow, blue glass orbs were used to support massive drifting deep-sea fishnets. By the 1970s, glass fishing floats were replaced by cheaper and lighter aluminum and plastic floats. Just like sea glass, the floats are increasingly rare to find, but a true treasure.

I could never stay long
enough on the shore.
The tang of the untainted,
FRESH AND FREE SEA AIR was like
a cool, quieting thought,
and the SHELLS AND PEBBLES
and the SEAWEED with tiny
living creatures attached
to it NEVER LOST THEIR FASCINATION
for me.

—Helen Keller, from *The Story of My Life*

III.

WHAT WE CAN LEARN FROM THE BEACH

The activity of beachcombing can be exhilarating. For example, when you have the opportunity to explore a new-to-you beach; when you come across a rare specimen and observe it, undisturbed, for several fascinating, fleeting minutes; or when you find a coveted treasure to add to your collection, perhaps after years of searching.

Beachcombing can also be incredibly calming. There is something about an aimless walk along an expanse of sea and sand and sky that is uniquely grounding. If you are lucky enough to come upon an empty, unoccupied beach—in the early hours of dawn, perhaps, or as a storm is brewing overhead—try to really

savor it. That is my favorite way to beachcomb: in total solitude, with no company other
than the sights, sounds, and smells of the
ocean. In our busy, modern lives, moments of
peace and quiet in the natural world are rare.

When I comb a beach or walk along the
shore, I often ponder life's bigger questions.
A seaside setting seems to invite this kind of
introspective thinking. In these next pages,
I've included a handful of the contemplative
musings that have arisen on my coastal adven-
tures; I'm sure you'll soon have your own to
add to this list.

OUR EXISTENCE ON THIS PLANET
IS RELATIVELY SHORT

Sometimes, we humans have grandiose
notions about ourselves. *We out-
evolved other species, we conquered this
planet, we reign supreme.* This is a myopic
perspective, however, that assumes evolution
has an ultimate goal (it does not) and that

we are the center of the universe (we are not). Remember that we came from the water, as all life did, and there are so many sea-going species that came before us and will outlive us. *Homo sapiens* have been around for a mere 300,000 years; compare that with the horseshoe crab (page 75), for example, which has existed for more than 250 million years and has barely needed to evolve to survive. These humble creatures may seem lowly, but in fact, they are extremely resilient, resourceful, incredible beings. Humans are a blip on this planet, and we would do well to remember that.

RESPECT THE ENVIRONMENT

We have but one planet to call home, and if we want to keep living here, we need to take care of it. About 71 percent of Earth is covered in water, most of which is ocean. Protecting our oceans is an essential step in saving our planet, and there are so many small steps you

THE TEXTURES
OF THE BEACH

Try this meditation at the beach, or simply imagine the beach and its many textures in your mind.

As you approach the sand, take off your shoes. Place one foot on the sand, then the other. Wiggle your toes and feel the grains of sand between them, scratchy and rough. Think how many tiny grains your feet are touching at this very moment—too many to ever count.

Walk along the shore and let the sand exfoliate your soles. The feeling may change as you get closer to the water. Notice if the grains become finer, softer, slightly damp.

Walk to the water. If it's safe, get close enough to the ocean so that the waves run over the tops of your feet. How does that feel? Is the water warm or cool?

From earth to water to air: Turn your attention to the air around you. Notice the temperature and how it makes you feel. Warm air may relax you, while cold temperatures may give you goosebumps. If there's movement in the air, whether a gentle wind or a gale, close your eyes and feel it against your cheek.

Finally, take a seat on the beach and let go of the busyness of your day. Focus on the moment and your ever-present breath. Feel your breath fill and then leave your lungs, your chest expand and contract. Sweep your fingers along the sand and notice the differences between the sand grains, how each one is unique in shape and size, yet still only a tiny part of the beach, which itself is a small part of the Earth's crust. Consider that you are yet another grain of sand on the Earth, a minute but important part of the whole. Carry this feeling of connectedness with you as you reawaken the rest of your senses in preparation to carry on with your day.

can take that add up to big change. Participate in a local beach clean-up, limit excess water usage, drink from a reusable water bottle, and minimize single-use plastic in your life. When you beachcomb, pick up any trash that you see in the surf or on the sand, and don't bother any living creatures that you encounter. Treat our Mother (Earth) with kindness.

LITTLE THINGS CAN HAVE A BIG IMPACT

Remember the humble oyster (page 47) and its ability to feed and shelter critters, protect coastal communities, and clean water at an astounding rate? The next time you encounter an oyster—perhaps at a restaurant or along the coast—remark on its small size and unassuming presentation. If you didn't know how much these little beings are capable of (and perhaps you didn't before reading this book), would you assume they were inconsequential? We have a tendency to judge a book by its cover, or in this case, an oyster by its shell. But as with many things in life, they are so much more than meets the eye.

TAP INTO YOUR SENSES TO GROUND YOU

Connecting with our sense of smell, touch, taste, or hearing is one of the easiest ways to ground ourselves in the present moment. In order to connect with our senses, we must first slow our racing thoughts. A beach walk—or any time spent in nature—is a wonderful way to do that. Forget that difficult conversation you had this morning, all the things you have to accomplish tomorrow, the endless to-dos and tasks. Instead, pause and pay attention to the here and now. If you wish, refer to one of the meditations in this book (pages 14, 22, and 120) to help you focus. You can tap into any of your senses, wherever you are, as a way to quiet your mind and reconnect with the world around you.

CURIOSITY CAN LEAD YOU
TO WONDERFUL DISCOVERIES

As children, we have so much innate curiosity about the world. We're constantly asking questions and learning new things. This cycle of asking and discovering ensures we keep growing and expanding. As we get older, however, our curiosity often wanes, whether due to busyness, arrogance, or routine. Beachcombing can be a wonderful reminder of how much there is to discover about this astonishing world and the oceans within it. With any luck, this book not only taught you something insightful, but also inspired many more questions. In beachcombing and in life, stay curious!

Burgard, Anna M. *The Beachcomber's Companion: An Illustrated Guide to Collecting and Identifying Beach Treasures.* San Francisco, CA: Chronicle Books, 2018.

Heller, Amy, and Gail Browne. *Lost and Found: Time, Tide, and Treasures.* Atglen: Schiffer Publishing, 2020.

Iselin, Josie. *The Curious World of Seaweed.* Berkeley, CA: Heyday, 2019.

Ricketts, Edward F., Jack Calvin, and Joel W. Hedgpeth. *Between Pacific Tides*. 5th edition. Stanford, CA: Stanford University Press, 1985.

Sept, J. Duane. *The New Beachcomber's Guide to the Pacific Northwest*. Madeira Park, BC: Harbour Publishing, 2019.

Vileisis, Ann. *Abalone: The Remarkable History and Uncertain Future of California's Iconic Shellfish*. Corvallis: Oregon State University Press, 2020.

Wye, Kenneth. *The Shell Collector's Handbook: The Essential Field Guide for Exploring the World of Shells*. New York: Wellfleet Press, 2015.

Zambello, Erika. *Coastal Life of the Atlantic and Gulf Coasts: Easily Identify Seashells, Beachcombing Finds, and Iconic Animals*. Cambridge, MN: Adventure Publications, 2021.